FIELD RECORDINGS

Poems by Russell Brakefield

FIELD RECORDINGS

Wayne State University Press | Detroit

ISBN 978-0-8143-4496-5 (paperback)
ISBN 978-0-8143-4497-2 (e-book)

Library of Congress Control Number: 2017949045

Publication of this book was made possible by a
generous gift from The Meijer Foundation. This work
is supported in part by an award from the Michigan
Council for Arts and Cultural Affairs.

Wayne State University Press
Leonard N. Simons Building
4809 Woodward Avenue
Detroit, Michigan 48201-1309

Visit us online at wsupress.wayne.edu

CONTENTS

I

II

III

We must view the folk song as the musical mirror of the world, as the primordial melody, which now seeks for a parallel dream image of itself and expresses this in poetry.

Friedrich Nietzsche

I

The Way We Learned to Sing

At the bar again, my back to the band,
     I'm listening for the quieter animal
   inside my body instead.

Outside—what passes from field to rot
     and back to snow—
   the ribs of March are kicking through.

And there are beasts bent across these hills
     that fill the night with praise
   for the natural order.

Who the elder mammal here
     and who newer?

Their howls scrape the black screen
     like a symphony warming.
   Each voice strays the pack

but is prepared to collapse together
     to sing the length of history's body.

A slip of land beyond the city's edge
     is threaded with ancient shadows,
   animals savage and famished

and put down like black patches on the snow
     as though they fell
   and their shapes, in falling,

opened room enough in the sky
for the stars to form.

This Is America and We Are Boys

We have been wild for so long now,
boyish and red with reminders
of the importance of acquisition—

a knife against the apple's skin,
the thin cycle of streetlamps on pavement.

Hounds are blessing the backs of buildings
we don't know how to leave,
blessing our exhaust breath. Ghost hounds,
back for the scraps.

Choose this vice or choose that, we say,
and count a tornado of slow concessions—
hives, inhibitives, acid reflux.

Choose this vice more than that, we say,
and find one heavy blanket to be enough.

When, in summer, we build a raft
of foam and rope and bend it into a thin river,
we know the statement we are making—

this is America and we are boys
slowly tiring into our fathers.

Our bodies are shorn and hung
with sly shadows. Our bodies hope
against the crack of armchair,
thick lung, hot chest.

The river, once dry then revived,
this is beauty we recognize
and destroy. A diorama,

slack edge of time, not knowing
what to do with even this—
just enough rope to keep ourselves alive.

The Butcher's Boy

Whitman's father was a carpenter
and conceivably also had boot-stained socks.

Mine, in the evenings, has his own beard
and copper foot stuck on the couch.

Hell hath no fury like a woman scorned, he says
and *Ask forgiveness, not permission.*

And I form the beginnings of a sorrow
that erupts and erupts in the presence of women.

My father's father was a butcher called Chuck
who died young and in the night,

his chest a suddenly collapsing fire,
the smaller kindling wrapped and eaten.

On the radio today—"The Butcher's Boy,"
a version that I can't recall

but do not doubt I've heard before.

Orchestra

Bees sleep
because they need to

like us. Together
a bundle

of bees asleep
at night

is a concertina
wheezing closed.

In the hive
they dance ,

a democratic dance,
a waltz

to prioritize.
Abdomen wobbles

a whole note.
I read today

some bees feel
the whir

of electric current
as they encounter

a flower's field—
bed of social

sparks, bed
of dying songs.

The Boy Whose Every Word Was Song

At first it was just birdsong,
    a garble or warble, a thin red thread
    worried from his throat.

At first only his parents felt the blessing
    and they kept tight lips, cherished their sleep
    and the hymnal fount they had birthed.

But no one stays a child forever,
    and in the streets these days
    he sends up a life-stained balloon.

As he walks his daily route—
    house to park to dark café—
    he speaks and the streets swell and tilt.

He's alone. It turns out
    few can stand a life swung through
    with constant serenade.

But strangers bloom around him endlessly.
    Children follow too close behind.
    The air above his head is licked with song.

And over the buildings and wires and flocks of birds,
    he makes a mirror in the sky that doubles
    the clamorous beauty of the living world.

Florist's Apprentice, Age 19

She was right of course, we are as much thieves
as we are divine, the horticulturalists among us.

Her hands unhooked the earth.
Swollen fingers nudged the roots
of a Mophead Hydrangea.

She was consummate at naming—
Moonlight, language plucked from history's catalogue
as she shook the cap in place
    and dragged atop a boggy sky.

And so I didn't ask, the summer I was her charge,
    when we scored lilacs on the Alden Highway,
who rightly claimed the stinky combs

cut in buckets in the truck bed. I loosed
bees and Japanese Beetles, fellow burglars
from our sour haul. Bunched pollen
    sparked on my jeans
through the fugitive light.

And later, deep in a mitt of euchre—
stowed lower deck—at the only bar for miles,
I would say—little thief—
to the beautiful bartender's daughter to my right,

Moonlight! Named for its lunar shape and glow,
for how it robs all the brilliant light of the universe.

Northern Michigan After Bar

Scrape of cotton to dirt and somewhere far off
the high bawl of pups, as we dip from our clothes
into the naked air and edge toward the lakeshore
where two black trays wobble against one another.

The group splits apart into disparate clusters,
buoys held waist-deep and limbed together.

I walk out on the water—a little Poseidon
with bad vision—and turn a wake into the darkness.
The others make their own small storms behind,
the shape of the night shrinking down around us.

Rag

Drenched leaf,
dragged and hung
beneath a bone of moon.

Undone by wind,
a walk-around dance
of rain and dew.

Do they know
what receptors run
these reedy troughs?

A lifeline burns
in each leaf,
inside my addled ears.

Through the window
raindrops sing
to the Beachwood.

Sleep unreels
its sloppy cadence
and wilts

the wound or heaven
or shadow guilt
I woke from.

The Ballad Form

in me is a sink full of empties.

Stones we pass over genetic pools
and on through reels of inheritance.

The way, as a child, Sunday mornings
always wore a light green dress—

gospel bluegrass on the radio
and my father coming back from the garden
hands stained, skin already mapped

red from the sun and work.

To know the successes of the household
by not knowing
the failures.

Diagnosis is the word we use
to signify illness
and origins.
What we inherit and translate—

short fuse or love of music,

restless leg syndrome,
some suddenly flaring trace
of chemical dependence.

Pardon, Trout Farm

A rafter of toms staggers the gravel.
Over the rearing tanks at dusk,
buckshot rattles the air and sends a panic
through the raceways. Other prey too
shudders with the light.

Spots dapple the pond top—
a spray of midges forging ore light
from the surface. Schools beneath lift
their ancient colors. Blades
of red, blades of silver.

The wind scrapes the soybean graves
back beyond the house. And inside
one light blazes—my uncle,
naked and close to the stove,
investigating again the mystic.

He knows when the rock burns down
is a cease fire for even the wilder kingdom.
No one's left owing anything to anyone.

Gate Keeper

I haven't had a comfortable dream
        in a dozen nights.

Each morning my mind
        throws a huge switch

and fills a room with sudden yellow light,
        sends the vermin back into hiding.

There are thirty-two liquor licenses
      in this town and as many other

back doors to walk into.

This morning, almost light again, the horizon
        sucks at the smokestacks
      as if they will begin to lift apart,

the buildings splitting in a rapture of foundations,
        a storm of rust

and bodies raining up
      against the sky.

Today I am a steel yard
        or that towering lumber company—

every troubled being moves into me,
        their hats and lunchboxes tucked at their sides.

Calendar Customs

And in the fall, as though all the windows felt
the coming necessity of support,
my mother lines their sills with glass jars.

A tomato fog creeps on the far walls
and runs silk scarves along the dishes
as they sleep in the cupboards.

She tells me she is hopeful. That despite the odds
I was born beautiful and my brother too.
And what is left to say to that?

She talks about her age and we stand
above the sink, the water red and too hot
for our hands. The dog outside barks at the wind.

Myth

To cut the knot of narrative,
drive to the outskirts and walk
towards a faint murmur of water.
Take no notice of the dance
at the river's edge
or the half-moon disco
of the two birds ahead.
One is not a macho Jay,
the other not a finch
cowering in fear. Driving,
ignore traffic accidents.
At home, turn off the television.
No sports coverage.
Forget reading. Beware, the brain
huffs stories like a teenager—
what's to be learned here
that will save me later?
Cut the lights and bag the glass
till you can't see your hands
before you. This dark
is not a precursor or ending.
Tell yourself. There's no lip of day.
There's no new light
waiting just out of reach.

After the Labor Day Procession

Tonight let's leave the others
    in the crowd,
        the smudge of street lamps

dimming behind our backs
    as we pass into the distant
        shadows.

Let's walk by the river
    where leaves cloud out
        even the Mill's bright lights

until I can no longer see
    the shape your face takes
        just before you speak.

If we walk slow with the bugs,
    down along the grassy bank,
        under that rib cage bridge,

we can catch a fat buzz
    off the night air, our cheeks
        like hard white shadows

as our eyes adjust.
    The cicadas have won over
        the echo

of the Main Street crowd
　　and the night unfolds now
　　　　as the softest dark toccata.

This dance we do together—
　　our limbs shift
　　　　to graze an arm or hand

against another's arm
　　or hand or the bright
　　　　bare knee emerging

from below your dress
　　that opens the sky
　　　　like the miniature moon

of some perfect little planet.

Minstrel

Like text book
planets, house

lights orbit
the bandstand.

I was born here,
long ago. Who

ripens in the wings
is gifted

certain flight. Like
memory, time

always happens
to music. A child,

I disrobed a fortune
teller and found

my own body
dancing,

dancing wildly
in the stage light.

Silent Movie with Playback Slowed Down

Unweighted by time, they float the hill
and emerge to thunder or the echo of thunder
that sets them counting. Her bare knees
are lit blue by a bolt released from its hutch
and made moment. Behind them, a mob
of white birch. Cut between, flashes of ink.
What he needs, he does not know,
and so the wheat, coy where it bows
to the night sky, is another enigmatic entry
in the book of all this. The wind and pinch
of wet grass it carries, a mystery. Her hair,
like a yolk of black horses, tumbles out in front.
Her skin is trapped moonlight. They fall
against the fork of a crabapple, where her thigh
will live on forever over his wet shoulder.
The night birds quiver. Like rain or time,
the field consumes them and the high grass
makes for them a furrow where they tangle
and turn to a single, nesting doe.

Barn Dance

The barn's wet with night
beneath bowed gambles.
A people heat spills
from the loft as we pass
the bottle between us.
Each body's a sun broke
from the stable's orbit,
from the fiddle's gambit.
Farther back the cattle tease
the dark with their own songs,
nipples aware the hour.
The milky moon settling in.
Because my allergy to bees,
their mumbling bodies,
the juice tastes brighter
in its danger, the night
made wild. The jug swarms
my grip as I tip it side-
long—*warm choke, chicken-
wing*, the old men say.
Glass lip ghosts my lip
like the moon, a waxwing
cut above us in the sky.

Rules for Recording Traditional Music, An Erasure

the machine   can do more
        The needle writes
            melodies,
      speech

                                    static

        can capture

                          confine the
living   Be-
tween songs

      forget   their   wish
           their home   their church
                       their person
                    The field recording

          is

                A funeral
          a wedding
              recorded

               his   voice comes
back   distorted   black mouth
                  that a child
     first recognizes   in a mirror

                                    prisoner

                        record

        record   finish

his voice

                    beat

                                                    to
        ghost

made
        convict

            a bucket
                                        a   murmur
    half   himself

River Song

The trout
   unlatched

to a blue-brown
   run of glass.

The baptism.
   The rocks

cloistered
   like eggs

beneath the surface.
   Flashes

of the visible
   spectrum

slink in their gravel
   windows.

This, our call
   and call back.

Our echo game.
   The rounds

we sing.
   I'm trawled

along the bed,
   ballooned

by rage and melt
   and the rest.

Distances Between the Head and Chest

1.

Value community and commodity
equally.

To know *these parts*—
            the way to the old farm trail,
which three men
to always find at the Alden Bar—
                is to know those parts—
capacitor, analyzer—
            as of the same hands, the same charge.

2.

Scratch the great lakes onto the insides of your arms.

Know a new idea of home

Know youth as finite.

The coastline eats time

like a tired
    child.

3.

Relativity is both special and general,
spatial
    `and a dark green shade spot along the ridge.

Nothing will move the mind
to punish the body

like memory,

like a single dissolving image—
the mill standing in the still cold morning air,
a woman's tiny feet inside flat canvas shoes.

4.

A sign of character is how you deal with failure.

OR

A slow giving up on
is the one true measure of subsistence—
    to examine regret like a small stone and then release it.

You cannot teach a dog to fake pain. You
    cannot deliver

your ownself
from the wreckage.

5.

Teach your children as if tomorrow
were already the day after.

Let their little bodies know the pleasure
of building a life on a night
      and a day   opening the same.

Along the river, the shadows
from the plant wires tower

like tall hunting birds.

6.

Don't talk about elevators,
the invention of the electric streetcar.

Burnt filaments hang

in the air   like tourists   in the streets.

7.

A man can be an eyelash
a wave

a boat
an anchor.

A man can be a blue bench
so far beneath

the brush
of a stand of box elders

that he barely exists.

A man can be a movie
of a different man

with the orchestra
breathing notes

hotly through him.

A man cannot be a poem
a river.

A man cannot be a pitcher
of cold water

a bent stem
a well

or anything that doesn't
move for fear

of standing still.

8.

If you lie about your upbringing do so often and with
confidence.

To see movement in the empty shop windows at night

is the same as to see the large magnolia tree

dipping fat leaves against your windows

until it looks like a father   or a furnace

or a first try.

Effigy

When the end has come, as is
fashionable to imagine these days,
and the land is covered with black
fog or retreating birds, their shadows
dwindled to bare and patchy masses,
the statues will inherit the earth.
The founding fathers will lurch
against the sky and finally take
their place as great distinctions—
white granite against a fiery lake.
In the yards of our childhood
homes, stone sparrows and frogs
crafted from long gone mothers'
hands will suddenly see themselves
alive in their brackish wading pools.
As it is, the past inherits us again.
As it is, Boston suddenly the most
populous city in the United States.
Wasp-wasted or gaining weight
from the city's sour rain, sleek
men and women, elbows no longer
stuck bent, will roam the streets—
the muse, a mirror of muses,
a boil of falling hawks. So many
dinosaurs and elephants. Spindled
lampposts alive like tyrant trees
and all the yards torn by their green
rust beings. Resurrection, as life,
is either sublime or it isn't—all
forgotten beasts are left to forage.

II

Alan Lomax, son of famous
ethnomusicologist John Lomax, was an
American folk music collector, archivist,
writer, musician, and oral historian. In 1938
Lomax set out on a three-month trip to the
Great Lakes basin to collect recordings
for the Library of Congress.

Field Recordings

"Am getting such grand stuff, I can't afford to leave."

~*Alan Lomax, Calumet City, MI, August 1938*

I'm making a verb of epigraph
so that my dreams embark
   in engravings.

This morning, upon waking, slow light
and a hymn held just off my tongue.

A parable wrung with sleep.
A song about white doves.

     »»

And then the tower of sound behind me.
Stuck husks of the neighbors I've known—

a thousand times a wives' tale,
a thousand times a myth

sewn through. The stories I'm told
   stick like reels below my ribcage.

     »»

Paramount has scouts picking the plains and south
from the blues on back. I've painted myself muddy
    on the map of all this.

I pick leavings, leave smudge shadows across the country
like war paint

like a fire anchored to a passing field.

        »»»

A tale of the five sisters—
each lays lake into the palm of the next
and between hangs a cradle, a lung, a corner
    untouched.

My father was lucky to settle south.
Best not to know the cooling kettle
set down here in the Midwest.

        »»»

The sun on the lake today is burnt
and brick, ruby running into butter.

Like the fat Firewheels of home,
fanned out behind the heavy shoulders
    of the Chrysler building.

I wear living rooms like raincoats.
I tango strangers like wives.

> >>>

Sing O' mountain spirits in Clairepoint.
The Serbian gusle calls you—
ballads played on bowed boats of central Europe.

Hands oar stories, line linens, lead labor strife.
Their nails run with coal crescents,

the sun sucked back the opposite way in the sky.

> >>>

Today, a shepherd's song runs me through
in double barrel

and after, the vertigo
    of wedding rites.

Hamtramck hums like a hive, a highball
    of history and radio.

>>>

The late night hustle is harder to shorthand—
.boot wine and rosin, three string and panel back.

The night frails open in smoky rooms.
I'm learning harmony again, that sneaky mask
    that lets me in.

Then a drunkard's sleep where I toss and jerk
like the needle's lurch, like I've just stepped down
off a sloppy boat deck.

>>>

In dreams I'm archiving innards
of the animals here

slick like orange rinds. I pull parts
toward my ears.

What's memory's myth.

I hear bears calling
from above, bodies shaken out
of all but stars.

A desert pup tails me from home.

Awake, the car's been robbed.

We hunt echoes, our ancestors
      hunt wolves.

                    >>>

Have found Hungary in Delray today—
Mrs. Mate's gay temperament, lent
and troves of lost sons from the old world.

I breach the waves of this inland sea.

My diving bell— a Presto, a net of wires and needles.

Caught adrift in my Plymouth Deluxe
with creoles which I did not expect.

            >>>

For the Library, I pick and mine.
I organize on vinyl and per diems
what will bare out of this land and its men.

The brain recalibrates experience for pleasure
and danger, we know this. And music, sung up,
rattles the lamp of history most.

>>>

Science lends us names for insight.
The crow knows endless faces

borrows and scrapes wood for forms
to fit up to a scrap yard cradle
riddled with others roosting.

And we say too what is held together by each other
is not lost to the elements—

feather, yarn, time   young. prayer, song.

>>>

The original diaphragm, the eardrum
hums like a cradle, burns needle rags
    into the brain.

Music transcends language, they say—each mother
marks the room the same color.

The womb is the first, best isolation booth.
Strung up with dark scarves, the heartbeat track
    lays deep beneath.

>>>

I'm counting loss in new ways—
equipment as memory, record as birth.

More theft means I've missed out
on a tent party in Inkster tonight.

The tale of my disasters here
is almost epic.

But then a Romanian laughing song,
loud and bold and honest,
waltzes through my brain again.

>>>

Some bedside lines—some fine, some simple
telegram signs— heading north, need more notes
for beer and bribes.

Or heading north, the wind
plays tricks on the eyes.

Hawks hold up the highway.

The coyote or the fox pisses the lakes
into existence.

>>>

On the road, a herd of early doe
hangs like eighth notes at the fence line.

Hawk-song. Screw wine of birch bow,
wound by the wind's torque.

And a mezzo shrike stifles a call
from its cage of hawthorn—

butcher bird, brilliant marauder—

twitches and withers
at the sudden turn of life on the air.

>>>

In the heart of the state spirits are sent on
through the water
    with lumber.

The way the creek becomes a river

becomes a lake if you aren't careful.

A rill rolls red with blood or a runnel without
beginning or end.

                              The creek runs a'howlin

                              Rolls in and never rolls out.

        »»

Even Paul Bunyan, it's said, not born in a mountain
but cut off the white pines

and hauled down the road
    to my microphone.

I'm taking shades of men's souls. Their stories
and my story, cut by the shadow song of theft.

        »»

For sustenance, not food but letters—

the lumberjack's alphabet covers loss and leisure,
scatter of limb and liver,

levels out living.

> *A's for axes swinging to and fro*
>
> *B's for the boys that handle them so*
>
> *C's for the chopping so early begun*
>
> *D for the danger the boys are all in*

>>>

A hymn for the new age—

we draw near dreamily
    dew cropped
    under the blade's green edge
    to the angels that light
    for each of us.

The road north swarms
with rows of grafted halos.

>>>

Taped, my own voice chirps, breaks
from the beak like a rodent's scrape.

On Union Street mouths rope with quilts of work.

A tree removed from the earth's dirt lips
amounts to meat, rings tallied until the tavern.

Each hoop holds coins, and then the old songs
run out like planks through a grinder.

              »»»

So many of these tunes are of a family
I know. Movement of people
or animals across land is called migration
    and also displacement.

A compression of air here is a slung stone
or feather blown there.

Anglers on the docks
hook swollen petals from the lake—
drift-wood, oar locks,
    nets packed with music.

              »»»

What is lost on what is passed on
on the tongue? The contours of song.

All art is an act of translation, is tactile.

The hammer tips the anvil in the ear.
The stirrup waits like a blind man in the canal.

Could call all this complicit, all knowledge

convict to the body

>>>>

On Beaver Island Drowsy Maggie
lifts the bones of Irish workers home.

A catgut bow furrows over the tinder of
an Irish fiddle. Song curls like kindling
and keeps quiet the worrying wind.

I catch it all in wire lungs.

Meanwhile, water, angry mother,
makes a nest of inbound hulls and masts.

>>>>

A story's wings are in its terror.
Tales tell here more eerily. Dock and harbor
   clap with specters.

The lake lays like a dripping page, anchors
cut by the wind, and chains

gone astray on the tongue. Brigs heft up
at eight bells and cast on unknown coasts.
Strung up in every legend—both elegy and boast.

      »»»

              They look out and she's running before a hard gale

              Upset went her rudder overboard went her sail

              Billows were forming like mountains of snow

              We'll never cross lake Michigan where the stormy winds blow

      »»»

In dreams now my memory is always off.
Light's housed in lesser light than I've known.

A part of sorrow is listening
to that you've heard before.

A bawdy song sung on one man's tongue
turns to lament on another's timbre.

Studding the shore of Lake Superior— bones
of a familiar Southern stag song.

>>>

Take your leg off mine

Take your leg your leg off mine

I ain't gonna tell ya but one more time

Take your leg off mine

Take your leg off mine

Take your leg off

Take your leg

>>>

Posen, near Cheboygan, holds a goldmine
in the sky. Polish children bring down rooms
a cappella, no autoharp to shake or trill.

Alto not choral, but the strains still cut through
like a heart attack on the bottom line.

These kids wear vocal folds like a sleeve.
Backup's played by a gold wreck of tamaracks.

>>>>

Recording is coded like language.
The cock throws his voice in the ring like a hat,
interrupts the short-drag for his misset clock,
      his come on early dawn.

The wives gone to bed, I fix another
lacquer cover, nitrate skin held over
aluminum. The hum and whir lock out the dawn.

>>>>

The road blows down from the north,
blows apart

hemmed with new blues
    because the season says.

A winter's letter, postmarked *enough!*

In dreams an old spasm band calls in.
Texas heat stalks me like a question.

Lovebugs turn out their catgut legs
    and cloud the radio lines.

      »»

And the road's its own song tonight.
Low back tire plays an offbeat.
Radiator rim shot. The horizon's grey
    like acetate

in the rearview. Rogers City moans
louder than any broken song
I've ever known.

      »»

Raked with white caps, the lake's wine
casts back

my old friend Potomac. In a letter
    home, read back,
        I'm lonelier than I thought.

No lead sheet for this lament.

>>>

Joked, a whale must live there
under Superior's dark blanket.

Told a whaler's tale now and sung a shanty
right at this hour, I would wear the monkey-belt myself

would take the blubber hook and fight.

In dreamlight, a baseball eye lifts off
    the sickly surface of the lake.

>>>

The shore collects with no remorse.
The wind adjusts the pitch

and leans into the birch trees'
accordion ribs, a wreck of carcass and drift.

Sea bird swings low
and writes a ledger line above the staff.

>>>

In Marquette the Iron pocket docks lurch.
I catch a parlor guitar's stitch, a gamut—
the word for it—of bicycles and garment shops.

The clumsy prison branch stoops.

In a clumsy pub an old iron man sits
    and tries to chase the root
        before the round comes back.

>>>

A wolf tone plays here in Baraga.
I'm beginning to think I'm Death's special herald.

The pitch of a father's passing is remarkable.
Locals mix French and English for this.

The night shakes out its own lament.
No knife guitar, no banjo, no bottleneck.

I run the devil and the devil runs me

I run the devil up the sycamore tree

Because pharaoh's army got drowned

Oh Mary don't you weep

»»»

Thumb string and open back, pattern picking like
Roanoke—

a scale length trails my Pontiac
and tempts me back out on the road.

In this Peninsula I'm no more minstrel than ghost,
   minor chord, blue note.

The wind plays me open on a mouth harp.

   》》》

The loon lifts her hooded head,
a red bead threaded in sidelong
along her awful bill and calls her spouse
across the turgid sedge mats.

Drove a hundred miles solo tonight
brooding over my clutch of discs.

At dawn, the decibel of waterfowl
is so unlike the radio.

>>>

Buckwheat or patent or sacred harp
the shape of a note starts with loss
or an arc of displaced air.

Preserve they say and mean repent.
Canon, cannon, ruin, contaminate.

I think I will do nothing for a long time now
but listen and accrue what I hear into myself
and let sounds contribute toward me.

III

The Wraith in the Creek

Pines felled
and undressed
of bows
are summoned
down the channel
through corsets
cut to run trunks
like silk. Ancestors
took work
where they could.
The creek is a thief
of its own.
Cloudy, the stone
that rests there.
As if current
weren't the most
constant force,
weren't eclectic,
weren't cursed.
In spring the gully,
suddenly swamping,
warns against
the sluice and
poach, rinses
the camp in red
and sends a wraith
beneath the surface.
Draw straws
for mercy.

In bunks
by lantern light,
bow heads.
Monkshood dips
along the water,
cat's tail and
helmet flower
all trod over.
Clover and carcass
dunked
and amphibious.
Call your gods
and if you're
spared be sure
to tell your children.
The ghosts on earth
take more
than the ones
below.

Mackinaw Island

"It is no more possible to predicate the conduct
of an Indian than that of a woman."
~*folklorist Charles M. Skinner in 1896*

In the picture, my younger brother hangs slack
from the stocks, his hands wrung by wooden shackles
like he were made for that time— unlikely colonial cap
tilted up on his tiny, hinged-in head. The island flattened
to a dream-map for us then. Fudge and high walls. Cap guns
hung like meat from the shop stalls. And just beyond,
my mother's hand cuts sun from her eyes, my father
behind the lens. Not content to live among a crate of plastic
bows and arrows—the swaying commerce of violence—
she has been made villain by her objection, made more foreign
to our little boyhearts. In another photo, in a schoolroom
diorama, she leans against a roll-top desk, shadowed
by the under-lit fort. I stand before her with a mock musket,
peering wildly down the barrel at my would-be savage captor.
The pitch from the log wall has stained her neck and hair.
She splays her digits out across a desk's surface, capsized
by silence, and traces scars cut deep into the dreamwood.

Nain Rouge, Red Gnome

The gnome came to him in a dream,
passed on as omen
in the bruise-blue pall of sleep.

Like all gnomes—a neologism,
a wrong fold of the tongue.
The game telephone, I'm told, is false
whispers elsewhere.

Awake, he was a man changed,
his ambition ripened
by the courage of facing small
and foreign gods.

So the name bloomed new fear—
Nain Rouge, Red Gnome—
and roamed like a song as it had before.

From the Cree and Ojibwa—
a man made of speech alone.
And so not unlike myself.

So you want the tongue of god, I read
again and again
in my college dorm room,
not to be godlike, but to exist.

The Dog-man from Luther

How many places are left in the woods where people still disappear?
Where those who do come down from the hills or out from the
mill-studded forest can only speak in a hush, voices rooted down to
the floorboards. At home tonight, dinner is a bird emerging from
its feathers, one crooked branch on a tree. I plan for these things,
the slow parts of the day, the way food can mask a different brand of
want. There must be a hundred dark pockets still out there—triangles,
quagmires, areas of unexplained disappearance. I hear the talk over
dollar beers at the Moose. Kids beneath the street lamps whisper and
make huge halos with their hands, hoist phantom saw blades into the
trees. They unshelve story after story—a zoo train turned on the pass,
a dozen wild animals loose on the Midwest winter, soot from the long
gone logging factory rising in the snowy air, hoards of beast men, the
Dog-man from Luther, packs of terror hot for a kill. Tonight I retreat
into these ghosts, a casualty of utterance or even the beast himself
with all his unbridled fulfillment—every day, blood like a hot new
coat on my tongue. I listen to the wind tonight for my name, set still
until it flickers like a candle in a wet cave. I let the whispers pull apart
my limbs and cast me deep into any story that is not my own.

The Girl with Birds for Hands

extends her arms as in trouble
or as though she's seen a far-off lover.

Call it all a plea for flight, every halt
or come hither is a feather
messing the blue air around her.

Barbs assign shapes to the weather.

In spring she digs for worms
by instinct, she uncovers a storm
of bodies writhing—the Boatman
unraveled on the sidewalk.

Hers is a real talent for undertaking.

At home, every caress carries potential
for collapse. Her bones, convicts
to their buoyancy, her palms
aflame with contours.

We see her on the street
and feel wealthy, the unknown
bowl of sky falling open again.

We see her on the street
and say *woman* and *wren*.

We feel mortal and grounded,
the wild world finally defined against us.

Raccoon Sighting Before Intimacy

He digs his rascal nose deeper
into the pit of pitch and mesquite,
a brick nest. His body contorts
like a dancer in the arms of a dancer,
backlit by a scattered clutch of charcoal.
I know this is not the best way
to say hunger, in each mask it wears,
is always of a desperate nature.
But here we are, both striped
in the evening light. I'm carved
by the slag of too much coffee
and watching all the small gods
of the porch swing. How at night—
when she undresses in the dark
and while I'm thinking of a book
or my brother or the trim loose
in the corner, while the clipped
blinds bang the window and harass
the last wasps snoozing in shudders
behind the house— I must pry
my instincts out of my body
and hold them like a fine
white sand in my fingers.

Habitat Diorama

Because the attraction to casual nests
of history, we see a pile of bones
and try to string its ligaments.

One beast, we say
though our eyes can count the many
femurs that lie like textbooks beneath.

The spectacle, someone says in the crowd,
as in an extraordinary exhibition,
an embarrassing situation, an aid
　　to intellectual sight.

The skull perched atop sees
nothing new. How we cover one life
lost and then the next

—action as ritual,
ritual as effacement. All the white

space wears down the body, wears close
encounters thin.

They moved the Eskimo
from the museum in middle school,
between trips,

and left us just hungry wolves.

Unreliable Auguries

cradled
by the slow turn of field.
As with the little tales

we are told and told
to tell. Little scrub jays,
start counting again.

Sheep, gather
in a puddle and foretell
the rain's dark edge.

And cows, lie down
and let us in on what little
futures you know too—

the strings that wind
back the skull
and tell the legs to bow

before the storm.
Let us imagine the forecast
of a chorus of bugs

spilling through the reeds.
As though it were
a daily answer

for suffering. Study
the crow's shoulders.
Do they break back

against the sky or tuck
low like a clump of stratus?
And saying what?

That a new voice stalks
beyond the hedge.
That the field stinks

of grouse and fowl.
A red moon runs
the dirt red too.

A low crop early
means a bad crop.
Dead hens in the field?

Look for the dog
or hawk or man
who was the hungriest.

The horse that lies
flat in the dirt pen
means, probably,

the horse is dead
or the horse is
almost dead.

Halcyon and Her Mortal Lover

In the trees today, the birds tremble
>   and anticipate the annual long division
> when they let half the self go mid-air
and sell their bodies to the wind.

Their breasts and wings enlarge
>   while their insides atrophy and unhinge.
> I can only say miraculous,
though others call it *the validation of quantum
entanglement*,

that each bird can see exactly where to go
>   and has such faith in something waiting
> when he lands.

Carnival Song

Does the Bearded Woman also know what it means to be forgotten?
Does she stir at night, a deck of cards folding and unfolding in her tiny
    stomach?
Does she sing the blues in a muffled voice as the stars turn on like
    mirrors in the trees?
Someone whispers in her girl ear, *To be is to be said, to have your name*
    held on the tongue of another
as if it were not for long there. As classification, she thinks, as distinction.
Does she know this, even in youth, a black wisp creeping across her lip?
Or never, only prayer after prayer for facsimile, for the hive's hot hum,
    single sun in the milk white stain of the Pleiades?
Harmony, she says, *is the best part of all.* To be in such agreement with
    the world that you are nothing and nowhere to anyone

The High and Lonesome Sound

> Who hears music feels his solitude peopled at once.
> ~Robert Browning

I. FIDDLE

We learn early to keep

    the most precious things close

to our necks— copper for health, jasper for beauty,

    a silver cross for faith or humility.

Onstage, the fiddle cuts the room open.

    Swivel stop of blade, the trouper's shoulder

swivels. A hand divides the torso.

    Scratch and bow, a steel drone scores

beneath the chin, unlaces the throat

    like a lover's fingers. Hair runs ruin, spins in

an act of revision. How we unfasten

    for stories of the body—bare limbs, perhaps,

made luminous by a mountain stream and tangled below

    the hum of lunar membrane.

II. BANJO

The hum of lunar membrane—

a minstrel mainstay. As each finger stands

for a region of the brain, each string played

cuts experience off the body. Part of the player

is leased to the listener like sign language or a farmer

swatting a barn cat from the butter dish.

A stage above the stage, the cavity rings.

Strings cluck and roll, pulse like veins. Inside

a sonnet dislodges to mucus. The octave stays alive.

Volta holds tight the heart of the gut-spun room.

A small bit of something—call it memory or music

or life— is carried through

to plume or skipper or ghost, is made

nimbler or more alive for the process.

III. MANDOLIN

Nimbler or more alive for the process

    the land clears again and again. Call this body

June bug—the belly blooms below the neck, moon

    stomach of a new mother walking barefoot

through a field of new wheat at night. Or the teardrop,

    more common, made soft to mimic the drip

in the strings an ancient soprano soundboard.

    Like angels, music descends a heavier,

more living self. Notes die quicker in the body, proof

    small spaces bend perception like light

through a shallow kill. The tremolo ruptures

    air like an echo-

ring print on the lake, the shake of each branch

    as each small bird leaves its perch.

IV. DOBRO

As each small bird leaves its perch,

    like the first reach of wren in spring—Peter Peter —

or the knock of the Pileated Woodpecker.

    These strings harrow and exhume

song from season turn, from timber

    torn lines and sunken boats. A boat its own,

the dobro's built to join others,

    a high strung harmony. The way all life

is born in the moments just becoming

    audible. One voice settles

to another and the resonator runs an ancient reel.

    Drop steel, hot howl, the room shakes

with string and vowel. A contra heat flares

    from deep below a sea of melody.

V. DOUBLE BASS

From deep below a sea of melody,

    some solid dub. Shoulders rub

a rosid back. The big body thumps. A neck

    like a highway, closet of sound,

the double bass knows empty space

    and nicknames well. *Upright, coffin,*

doghouse, bull fiddle—rhythm's an anagram,

    rearrangement of all the names

you know. *Contrabass, wash tub, bass violin.*

    Beneath the rest the bass sweeps

the floor of leavings, names

    the music's shadow breath

and gathers up grace—that staggering ghost—

    like a collection plate.

VI. GUITAR

Like a collection plate

    green beneath a Sunday's weight

the guitar's incurves rake in hymn

    and soul. A retronym, a wide-bodied vault

for whole generations of *want tos* and *somedays*

    and just beyond the fence lines.

Stories balloon inside this resonant cavity—

    chords cut like flesh off the world's

workers, skinned off their backs and struck

    from the sneaky palm of history.

The arched top opens to a wooden channel,

    a machine made to fill dead air, a field

where we hunt the scraps of ourselves

    we are taught so early on to keep.

Fermata

En route to Kalamazoo,
we tracked the half-drunk animal between us.
Center-pivot watering lines crawled along beside us.

Out the windows, time towed silos
and haylofts toward the weeds,
the corn corn gone rot and cut below the knees.

My brother and I shifted in our seats
and let in the rush of August wind
to bark away the silence then.

A sunk back mare swayed alone
behind a docile crib—swift farewell
before the concrete lid rose around the city.

You can just drop me anywhere, he said,
like a conductor setting down his baton.

Ode to Joy

Frank O'Hara

Slats hammered in along the tree limbs
form a skeleton for the kids to climb.
I've waited all day for this light—orange fog
above the pond where all life lifts away.
Behind the shed, memory of a dog's shaved
aside the grass. His lead hangs like a downed noose.
Bare ground, littered with bones, is poached
by the same light that grips me now
through the Ironwoods. I flounder
on the porch to belly the sail of a poem
I once knew well—not the child who's alone
in the schoolyard and not about the sudden snow.
Some kitchen music breaks out the screen door
like a platoon of geese cutting the air.
And with it comes the song I was looking for—
near the grave of love / No more dying.

Shutter, Lag

Driving, we saw a shepherd swollen to the shoulder
    and I told her it was a deer.

The smaller ones, I said, are here for the thaw.

A backdrop of cattails watched over the bloating.
    A ceiling of glowing lilies.

In the movies sometimes a person will close his eyes very
quickly.
    A snap of shutter, a lag. An open window
    closing.

At night I dreamt I could wave my limbs and lose them.
That nothing was the worst thing to be.
Then that I was a ship builder, my hands filled with wooden cells.

I woke and wrote and wrote.
I worked like a magician at a child's party,
    towards a mastery of disappearance and creation.

The animals I can't name, I can kill off or invent.

The swallows in the attic brushed their wings
against the tresses like white gloves, and she slept on
    in her nest of blankets.

Some days we still wake so close
you could not convince me of our separate dreaming.

Morning Song

Today I am a bee
burrowing into a glass
jar of honey

recognizing finally
a sweet, still pool
of my own making.

Ruby Creek Road

Michael's body, boyishly thin and still April pale, running bare along
the path to the Ruby Creek Road, reminds me of a dozen little things
I thought I had forgotten—berry picking, pollywogs, a dozen black
daubs of life crushed inside my palms, the cold crease of water after
running fast enough for long enough to let go of fatigue completely.
The power lines above us hang like two metal terrors, held at the ready
for a game of cat's cradle, make a sound like sun, and Michael's boy
wants to know Does energy lost in this way also become something
gained elsewhere, by an other? A speeding ticket from the state
highway hangs on the back of my head— a wet leaf stuck along the
banks of the moving water, and tomorrow's work is so close it blows
in hot below my eyelids. Later, back at the farmhouse, Evan and Mary
will make beans and chard and the harder light of the day will move
like a slow rolling stone over the sky. There is a good chance I have
done many things wrong in my life, to have landed here only just now,
to see a bantam move loudly across the yard, to watch the pull of the
grass in the wind, and to be thinking about something else, something
far off and completely different.

Kalkaska County, Michigan

I want to be this close or closer
for the rest of the night, hung

among the docks stored for winter
in the top of the garage. Our legs

are knives below the sheets,
wet blades awake in the ability

to seem briefly congruent,
sharp and handled.

In the morning, our heads still
cobwebbed, we will hunt mushrooms

in the dew and leaves
along Morrison Road,

consoled by our quiet looking,
the necessity of space apart

below the sparse, dark trees.
Our heads bowed like children

at the altar, held close to figures
most beautiful in their strangeness

and you will say, *I think I've found one.*
I think this one is real.

Wedding Song

for Ben and Megan

A crane banks, frenzy of wing beat.
Then another breaks the glassy finish—

stalks tucked, then untucked.
The sky's gone chalk. A day-moon

hung up in its socket. A dissimulation
of cranes— as in *pretense*

or as in *concealment*— unreels, distinctions
brushed from a larger particular,

a siege unhinged in a meadow of sedge
and burr weed. One lifts his ruddy wings

in banter. The other buckles her
brilliant head and sings across the mat.

The cattails dip in chorus. A contra,
two step, the cranes bob and slip.

The wind rocks off the marsh
and calls a gentle blessing forth.

The Perseids

Eyes aloft in August, lifted towards the East.
I am hoping for a flurry, radio dust
stretched across the night sky.

Above me, all the alien lovers are asleep,
stuck together beneath their foreign moons.

There is a woman at home in bed with her dog.
She knows I'm looking for the Perseids.
I've reminded her the time is now to go out
and gather the oldest fires of the universe.

Each time we order a group of stars
we invoke great empathy
for the living forms around us.

The comets are quiet still and I am a tree,
blacker than the sky or the dirt.

Were she with me, I would move my hand around her waist
like the sun of some long dead globe.

I would tell her how Perseus turned titans to stone,
struck down snakes and beasts of the sea
for his Andromeda.

I can find no greater source of envy—
he who crossed the world for his love,
to be pressed together for eons in the sky.

Origins

In the beginning all art was audible.

This accounts for the sea in the shell,
the cupped hands of echoes,

ears held against the gravel ground.

In Chauvet and El Castillo, the stomp of hooves.
In Gua Tewat, the scrape of praising palms.

Pictograms still play tight toccatas
in the Cumberland Plateau.

Every man's condition is a solution
in hieroglyphic.

Every man's a shadow song.

Across cultures, cave paintings hang
in concentrated stains
at the points of best acoustic resonance.

Stone and time hides a sonic canvas.

An atlas of first notation

where the pulse clinging to the rocks
renews itself forever.

NOTES

"Rules for Recording Traditional Music, An Erasure" was composed from a text by Alan Lomax of the same name.

"Field Recordings" is based on the life and writings of Alan Lomax. The language right justified in italics is from the folk music collected on this 1938 trip to Michigan. The line "I'm beginning to think I'm death's special herald" is taken directly from Lomax's journals. The line "We hunt echoes, our ancestors hunt wolves" was given to me by Benjamin Fidler. The poem ends with a line from Walt Whitman. This poem owes a great deal to the resources made available by the Library of Congress.

"Mackinaw Island" is after Adrienne Rich.

"Nain Rouge, Red Gnome" takes a line from Major Jackson.

"Habitat Diorama" was influenced by a painting titled "Bones" by Siobhan McBride as well as the performance art of Tanya Tagaq.

"Ode to Joy" ends with a line from Frank O'Hara

"Origins" takes a line from Ralph Waldo Emerson and a line from Louise Bogan.

ACKNOWLEDGMENTS

Grateful acknowledgment to the editors of the following journals where some of these poems first appeared: *Bluegrass Today, The Collagist, Crab Orchard Review, Hobart, The Michigan Poet, Midwestern Gothic, New Orleans Review, 3288 Review, Southern Indiana Review.*

Thank you to the Helen Zell Writers' Program for supporting my writing and teaching. Thank you to my incredible teachers Laura Kasischke, Keith Taylor, Khaled Mattawa, Mark Yakich, Van Jordan, Kim Chinquee, and Robert Fanning. Thank you also to Peter Ho Davies, Michael Byers, Doug Trevor, and Jeremiah Chamberlin for their continued support. Thank you to Michael Delp, Joe Horton, Raymond McDaniel, Aaron Burch, Joshua Edwards, Lynn Xu, Franke Varca, John Ganiard, Mike and Hilary Gustafson, Chris McCormick, and Mairead Small Staid for their guidance on this manuscript and for their friendship.

Thanks and many free burritos to my winter/sessions brothers. Thank you to Seth Bernard, Earthwork Music, and to Camp Greensky. All my love and gratitude to my best friend and partner Aubrey Schiavone, and to my writing buddy Bella.

Thank you to John Ado and to my parents, Jeff and Chris— this book is for you.

ABOUT THE AUTHOR

 Russell Brakefield received his MFA in poetry from the University of Michigan's Helen Zell Writers' Program. His work has appeared in *Indiana Review, New Orleans Review, Poet Lore, Crab Orchard Review,* and elsewhere. He has received fellowships from the University of Michigan Musical Society, the Vermont Studio Center, and the National Parks Department.